RAISING BETTER CHILDREN

Key To Effective Parenting

CHRISTINA CHITENDERU MTHOMBENI

Order this book online at **www.trafford.com**
or email orders@trafford.com

Most Trafford titles are also available at major online book retailers.

Printed in the United States of America.

ISBN: 978-1-4669-5762-6 (sc)
ISBN: 978-1-4669-5761-9 (e)

Trafford rev. 10/17/2012

 www.trafford.com

North America & International
toll-free: 1 888 232 4444 (USA & Canada)
phone: 250 383 6864 ♦ fax: 812 355 4082

DEDICATION

To my beloved daughter Tanya Kagiso, who gave me the pride and joy of being a parent, each time more enchanting and a delight to our eyes. My late mother Rose, for the infinite values she instilled in me, love and most of all believing in me. My dad Samuel Dennis for the care, the jokes, the laughter and all the family moments we share. To my love Courage, for the love and care and everything . . . .

My siblings Bertha, late brother Barbs, Helen, Emmanuel, Kenneth, Verna, Chitsva, Josie, Rashma Gee and their beloved families. My nieces and nephews. My friend Sonia Searle for being a very constructive friend-always positive.

Rowa United Methodist church and the whole community, where I grew-up and moulded into who I am today. The Luton Central SDA church, where I worship and fellowship.

Acknowledgements

To the most divine power that makes all things possible, God for making this project possible.

Pastor Chackochen and family, for the encouragement and support. My beloved families for always standing by me and helping me where i need.

Betty Makoni, for the inspiration and strength that comes from her background and rising above situations.

Many thanks go to everyone else who has contributed positively in my life.

INTRODUCTION

I wrote this piece, not because I am the perfect parent, not because I possess greater knowledge of parenting, not because I can write . . . . the inspiration came from the mere knowledge that as a parent, it is not by being clever or educated or in being in the best or worst of circumstances but simply that, every parent is entrusted with this responsibility.

As we move into this journey of parenting, we sometimes stumble and many a times we don't know what to do and the most difficult moment in a parent's life is when one is faced with a situation and do not know what to do, where to start or how to face it. It's like a child is looking up to you with hope and trust but you have no idea what to do.

Every parent will be faced with different challenges during their course of parenthood. Some challenges pushes us to the wall that we might give up and feel that we have failed. It's very easy to feel the sense of failure when faced with challenges but being a parent is rising above these situations and making the best out of it.

When we had our baby, my husband and I were overjoyed, rather ecstatic and looking at the tiny sweet baby was . . . . quite overwhelming.

I can say I had tears of joy and at the same time a wave of nervousness. The reality kicked in and the lifetime commitment had just begun, the responsibility to provide and nurture this blessing. One sure thing amidst all this happiness was, we both had no idea where to start, how to take care of the baby—not even how to bath her because she looked so fragile and we didn't want to hurt her.

Being far from our families, our friends and other relatives who had children played a vital role in assisting with advice and some important tips on taking care of the baby. Sometimes we would call at midnight when the baby was crying nonstop and we would always get all the reassurance that we needed. The most difficult phase passed and up until now we still get good advice on parenting from families, relatives and friends.

In a nutshell, this book serves as a handy guide or advisory tool to parenting on a few topics that I have had exposure through my studies, work and the society In general. It gives summarized points which can help and guide every parent to a better outcome in this journey. Short and precise, also friendly to parents who lead busy lifestyles.

The content in this piece is not specific to any age group, ethnicity, religion, sex or race. It out surfaces the general psychological needs for parents and children, it's more of a neutral material, of course in some parts there can be more emphasis on maybe teenagers, toddlers or grown up children.

In my mind when I thought of writing this piece, I also carried in it those parents out there who might be in a Limbo situation where they are like on a crossroad and have to act quickly but they have no idea in the blue what to do, where to go or let alone how to.

It comes with great pleasure to share no matter how little the information might be, we might be surprised how even one word can completely change someone's life, the power of words, so little and yet so big. We survive by words, written or spoken, words can change lives and in this book, it's just a few words but words from my heart to your heart.

I remember vividly one incident, It was my first few months in a Portuguese speaking country and I went out for coffee with a lady who was my colleague, she didn't understand English and at that time my Portuguese was as bad as not speaking.

Surprisingly we chatted and I could understand what she was trying to say and she could understand me too, I don't know how but I remember her story was, I've just went through divorce because I could not conceive, so the words that made me understand her whole story was the two key vocabulary words that are similar to the English *divorce—divorcio* and *conceive—conceber*, these two words made me understand the whole story.

After about 6 months, my Portuguese had improved and I invited her to my apartment and this time we could understand each other and I confirmed the story she was relating to me some months back. You might not read the whole book but take a few key words with you.

CONTENTS

Raising Better Children: Key to Effective parenting

Parenting is an immense fulfilling experience per se, it gives every parent the joy and pride of parenthood, the drive to work harder and be of good conduct. Being a parent on the other hand can cause grief, paranoia, stress, hurt, anxiety and more. To a larger extent, sometimes parents wish they could one day wake up to a parenting manual that by just following the steps you automatically achieve your aspirations. It is unfortunately not achievable because parenting entails surprises like poetry, capable of taking your breath away momentarily.

The majority of parents desire their children to do best in everything, in school, at work, in the community; every parent wants obedient children, respectful, hardworking, and intelligent and all the good things that a person can possess. When they grow up and ready to have relationships and marry, parents expect children to bring home fine young men/ladies, intelligent, hardworking, loving, respectful, but they might bring the worst nightmares—drug addicts who walk around with unkempt hair, ex-convicts, rumored prostitutes and all the worst characters you can think of.

Parenting is a lifetime commitment, starting from the day they come to the world until we part through death there is no day that passes without a parent getting concerned or rather think of their children. The challenges are dynamic and they change in the corridor of time. We can in a nutshell call it a bittersweet journey of parenting.

Main Challenges Faced by Parents:

- Disrespect
- Promiscuity
- Disobedience
- Lying
- Cheating
- Stealing
- Drugs
- Alcohol intake
- Bullying
- Pre-marital sex
- Gangsterism
- Bad company
- Modern Technology

These challenges can be largely influenced by environment, society, upbringing, friends, and personal choices e.t.c. Most of these challenges are what we see every day in the streets, at home, neighbors and in schools.

To add on to that, parenting in the 21st century comes with even more challenges that the parents more than 20 years ago did not have to face, including the internet and cellphones, as well as the decrease in the number of traditional two-parent families. According to a 2009 Federal Interagency Forum on Child and family Statistics report, the percentage of births to unmarried women rose from 18 percent in 1980 to 40 percent in 2007.

PARENTING STYLES

There are four basic parenting styles according to Diana Baumrind, a clinical and developmental psychologist. The parenting styles clearly explain the way parents differ in their approach to parenting, the pros and cons of each type of parenting. However, I believe there are more parenting styles out there yet to be explored. The fourth parenting style which is the Uninvolved/Neglectful Parenting was an expansion to Baumrind's three styles by Maccoby and Martin

1. Authoritarian Parenting (Too Hard)

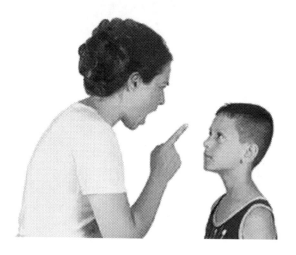

This type of parenting, children are expected to follow strict rules established by parents. Failure to follow instructions and rules results in punishment. In most cases if asked by a child why this or why that, they simply say because 'I say so'. Authoritarian parents fail to explain or rather justify the rules that are put in place. According to Baumrind, these parents are obedience and status oriented.

Example:

The parent tells a child, 'I want you to play soccer in school as your choice of sport', but does not bother to ask the child if they have interest or are good in that sport. Even if the child expresses discomfort in it, the parent persists and even goes on to buy the soccer attire. This kind of parent imposes in the child's life.

2. Authoritative Parenting (Just Right)

Authoritative parents establish rules and guidelines that their children are expected to follow. This parenting style tends to be more democratic. Parents are responsive to their children and are willing to listen to children and make calculative response. When children fail to meet expectations these parents are more nurturing and forgiving rather than punishing. They are assertive but not intrusive and restrictive.

Example:

The child says, "I don't enjoy the Maths subject and I'm not so good at it, i always get below average mark". The parent says ok, you can concentrate on the subjects you find interest in and the ones you are good at. They do not make an effort to see if they can do something that can help like hiring a private tutor or doing group work with friends who are good in Maths.

3. Permissive Parenting (Too Soft)

These parents are sometimes referred to as indulgent; they have very few demands to make to their children. These parents rarely discipline their children because they have relatively low expectations of maturity and self control. These parents are more responsive than they are demanding, non traditional and lenient. They do not feel the need for mature behavior and they avoid confrontation. They are generally nurturing and communicative with children; often take on the status of a friend than that of a parent.

Example:

The child goes out with friends to the movies or to the park. The parent does not say what time they are expected to be home, with whom is the child going to hang out with and how long the activities take. They just leave the child to go as long as they say I'm going out, no further details are due to the parent.

4. Uninvolved/Neglectful Parenting (Don't Care)

An uninvolved parenting is characterized by few demands, low responsiveness and little communication. While these parents fulfill the child's basic needs they are generally detached from the child's life. In extreme cases, these parents may even reject or neglect their children.

Example:

The child cries for hours and hours, the parent does not care to check what is wrong with the child or what do they need. This kind of parenting also surfaces laziness both mental and physical laziness.

- Authoritarian parenting styles generally lead to children who are obedient and proficient, but they rank lower in happiness, social competence and self-esteem.
- Authoritative parenting styles tend to result in children who are happy, capable and successful.
- Permissive parenting often results in children who rank low in happiness and self-regulation. These children are more likely to experience problems with authority and tend to perform poorly in school.
- Uninvolved parenting styles rank lowest across all life domains. These children tend to lack self-control, have low self-esteem and are less competent than their peers.

Food for Thought
1. What bracket of parenting do you think you fall in?
2. Do you think it's possible to change you parenting style if you realize that your parenting style is not effective?

TIPS TO UNDERSTANDING YOUR PARENTING STYLE

- Get Feedback from children or spouse, they spend quite a significant amount of time with you, so they know you better.
- Attend parenting courses in your area; it helps to share parenting experiences with other parents.
- Examine how you were parented and see how that had an impact on you.

Understanding Children

Children's Perception

Perception in children is the capability to identify and understand the meaning of actions, words and expressions. This is largely influenced by the different environments that they are exposed to; the lifestyle they lead at home; basically the way parents or guardians behave, talk and express themselves.

Children develop their character and behavior based on what they perceive as life through what they see, hear, do e.t.c. For example most of the children who come from violent backgrounds where parents resolve issues by fighting in front of the children, raise their voices all the time tend to understand violence as the only way to solve problems in life because they understand no other way. Unless they learn a better approach to life, they will think violence works because their supposed role models, the parents use that.

The children who come from parents who use dialogue at homes, create a loving and nurturing environment, are most likely to follow these steps as well because they are exposed to a harmonious environment.

Children are color blind when they are young, until they hear and see what the adults comment about people, situations and life, be it about their race, ethnicity, sexuality, religion. The power that the parents have in moulding children is quite enormous that the ball is left in their court to use the power into great transformations or worst outcome in the children.

Sometimes parents insult children or do not use very appropriate language to them, and most times it becomes a routine that at the end the parent seizes to understand the negative impact of such words for example where I come from, most people use the word '*pfutseki*' a lot and this word is not a polite word, it is derived from the Afrikaans language, '*voetsek*' meaning 'get away' mainly referred to a dog. Because parents continually use this word, every child grows up using it.

Everything we do at home, in front of the children is an investment because that will live with them forever; it will contribute to moulding their character, behavior and personality. We are investing by the way we conduct ourselves i.e. being loving, being respectful, being cheerful, gossiping, shouting, fighting, hating, cheating, disrespecting.

The consequences might not surface today but can manifest 20 or 30 years later. It is quite pertinent for a parent to ask themselves, 'what kind of investment do i want to leave for my children? This is not a material investment but a personal, emotional, character, attitude, behaviour investment.

Children's Emotions

HAPPY SAD ANGRY

CALM SCARED SURPRISED

The mainstream definition of emotion refers to a feeling state involving thoughts, physiological changes, and an outward expression or behavior. Like adults, children also have emotions right from the minute they come to the world, they can be happy emotions or sad emotions and mostly in children sad emotions are shown by crying, being withdrawn or failure to talk or communicate. Happy emotions are mostly characterized by laughter, smiles and being playful.

This is normal and parents have a responsibility to make sure that what they say and do does not make a lasting negative emotion to their children but lasting positive emotions. Most children misbehave and can be a handful at times, this is also normal but if a child does wrong, we must be careful what we say and how we say it to them to avoid saying things that will affect them for a longer time. It is important and pertinent to discipline the children accordingly but we must not be condescending to them especially in front of other children or peers.

This is an account of an eight year old boy, this young boy was very intelligent, loving and obedient to his parents and the teachers at school had a high regard of him. The parents were proud of him, he always came first in class and he worked hard at school and at home. This young boy was a dream of every parent.

At the end of his third term, for some reason he failed the Content subject and this resulted in him not coming first in class as he used to.

As he was disappointed in himself, the parents were even more disappointed in him that their young boy had failed. The mother told him immediately after seeing his report," oh, young boy you are becoming lazy and useless, this is not acceptable". This hit him hard and the two words that most affected the young boy were lazy and useless. From that day on he felt that her mother looked at him as a lazy and useless boy, so he lost the drive to do good to the extent that he even perfomed worse in school and at home.

Building the Children's Self esteem

Self esteem is personal confidence, the capability to understand yourself and what you want and not be afraid/hesitant to express yourself in your most comfortable way. Self esteem is not feeling ashamed of yourself, no matter what you are going through, what transpired in your past or where you come from. Many a times children are daunted or intimidated by other children or rather they feel they are not good enough because they don't know their biological father or mother, they live in a small house than their friends, they are not dropped at school by car, they only have one pair of shoes or non at all.

This can hinder many children's success and doing something good with their lives. This aspect also comes back to the children's background, it is quite vital for parents to assure their children even if they do fail in doing something. Even if you don't have what the neighbors have, even if you can't afford a bicycle—teach children to rise above the situation and be happy and content, make them feel satisfied and proud of themselves.

The role of a parent is to constantly remind the children how good and confident they are by praising them when they do little tasks at home or at school, it's the small things that create bigger achievements. The life they lead is also a big self esteem booster; children who live in harmonious families tend to have better self-esteem than those who come from abusive or violent families.

Lack of self esteem can also lead children into lying, stealing, jealousy, promiscuous and more.

In Northern Namibia, there is a very fascinating community of the Himbas, they are from the Herero Tribe. The Himbas live in mud houses and they only wear animal skin to the front and the back, the women don't wear any blouses or t-shirts which exposes their breasts. They apply a traditional cream that tans their skin and they walk proudly even though they are constantly exposed to people who dress up completely.

This is their culture and they are proud of who they are to the extent that many tourists go to that community to visit and take pictures because they are peculiar, whilst others are competing to see who wears the best and expensive clothes, the Himbas are captivating more people by just wearing animal skin half skirts and nothing on top.

In high school most young children's fathers are bank managers but in most cases not even one of them is, this is highly contributed by parents who are not proud of who they are and what they do to support their children.

If you do menial jobs to support your children and you always say I wish I could be somebody better and yet you are providing the necessities for your children. Yes it is important to think bigger for the future but don't feel ashamed of what you are today. It does not matter what you do, let your children know that you are doing a good job by making sure they are well provided for.

A good example of good self esteem, my husband and I were one day watching a reality TV programme about two teenage girls in Russia, who were abducted and kept in a basement for four years being used as sex slaves by one man who apparently did not have self esteem.

It was so painful for us to watch because we were trying to imagine the hurt and grief that they were going through. Whilst they were in captivity, one of the girls realized her skill in art, drawing beautiful pictures and some of them that depicted the situation that they were in.

Surprisingly, they managed to trick the enslaver into trusting them and give them a bit of exposure to the outside world, they managed to sneak in a small note to one young lady to let her know that they were kept in a basement. This enabled the police to go and rescue them. They were finally free after four years of torture and grief.

The most humbling and touching part is how these young girls managed to bounce back from the predicament, they both refused psychological help which was sponsored. They refused therapy because they felt they did not need any therapy as they were prepared to move on and be happy as life is too short. We did not expect that response but it is a lesson for many young children out there, learning to be resilient to adversities.

Ways to Build The Children's Self-Esteem

- First improve your own Self Confidence As a parent by understanding and accepting who you are.
- Heal your past, no matter how bad it can be.
- Play with your children
- Make your children feel special
- Help your children develop talents and acquire skills
- Keep a kid friendly home
- Give children responsibilities
- Encourage children to express themselves, not bottle up their feelings

1. Do we have self esteem?
2. What are we doing to build our children's self esteem?

ENCOURAGING CHILDREN— SELF DEFINITION

Developmental stages of children pose different challenges and mainly it is because they are trying to adapt to the particular new stage. Children are different in many ways and as much as they are born and groomed by the same people, they each possess unique characteristics. For example, most parents tend to think that the only way for children to be successful is academic excellence in school. Of course academic excellence is a very important key to a better life but there are children who are generally not academically good, no matter how hard they try, it is still difficult for them to get it.

It is therefore the parent's responsibility to identify your child's *forte* (strong points), you might be the parent of the next Technology guru like Bill Gates, business moguls like Lord Sugar, athletes like Usain Bolt, talk show queen Oprah Winfrey . . . who don't hold PHDs in terms of academics but they are even more successful than the most educated people.

When parents realize that their child is not doing well at school, the words that usually come are: I want you to perform like Susan did, the neighbor's child she performed very well in class, why don't you do like her". Yes, it is important to take inspiration from others, but it is a different issue when we want our children to be like someone else because they are not.

Instead of dwelling much on the neighbors' child, let's try and identify what our child is really good at and try to nurture that. It is painful for parents to see their child come last or performing really bad in class but let's not make it worse by further discouraging the child because they feel inferior just by you mentioning that someone else is better than them.

It is very important to encourage our children to do well and to do good, even when they do the smallest gestures, they deserve a wow and that wow will encourage them to do more good because they want to hear that many times. This also goes to everyone even adults, for example if your boss tells you, you have done an amazing job at any particular task, the next step is to do more because you want to hear that more often, those who have spouses or partners, if your spouse says wow baby you are looking gorgeous, you obviously try to work more on yourself. Positive words have a very strong effect in one's life.

Let's encourage our children to be respectful; honest, loving, giving e.t.c.This brings us to the next sub-topic Self Definition.

Self Definition

Many children are in an identity crisis especially the teenagers because they are in that important transition from childhood to adulthood. A lot of feelings and emotions play a big role in them. It is very important as children are developing and growing in our eyes to teach them how to define themselves.

Self definition is when one sits down and contemplates on what kind of a person they want to be, how they want people to regard them. There are very few people who take time to do this but it helps the children to know their limits and identify their weaknesses. Self definition helps you to reach your full potential without much disruption from external pressure.

Young people can define themselves by saying I want to be obedient, respectful, hardworking, modest in my dressing, abstain from sex till marriage, I don't want to hang out with friends who abuse drugs and alcohol . . . . the list can go on. This is different from saying I want to be a Doctor or Lawyer, it is more of a character, conduct, behaviour moulding tool.

How to help children define themselves:

- Find a conducive time and environment to talk to your child, if you have more children make time for each one of them separately.
- Show love to your child as you speak to them, they mustn't feel like they are in the principal's office.
- Ask your child, "who and what do you want to be', this does not refer to professional achievement.

They might find the question a bit tricky but listen carefully as they speak, for every good point, show that you are pleased and give some assurance. This exercise gives a child the sense of responsibility and the will to execute what they have said. This talk can be done as soon as the child starts talking and understanding things. E.g the infants can talk about not refusing to bath, eat or sleep on time. This goes with a lot of prompting especially with infants. Parents should then help maintain these values that the children put forward as their self-definitions.

It is difficult to waver from what you have said. When I was single,I defined myself based on challenges faced by single girls, I knew my limits and what I wanted in life, I comported myself based on how I wanted the next person to treat me. When I got married, my principles changed too because I have someone in my life and I defined how I want to comport and what the most important things in marriage are.

1. Have you had exclusive time with each of your children?
2. Do you think self definition is important to children as well as parents?

Communication Skills

Communication is key and the basis to every relationship, parent—child, spouses, siblings, work e.t.c. I said communication skills because it is actually a skill, it does not happen easily, but it can bring either negative or positive implications and it has the capability of building or destroying relationships.

The way a parent communicates with the child is important, for example if a parent is abrupt when trying to make a point to a child; obviously the child might not understand and will get even more confused. It is vital to make sure the way you talk and the words you use are understood by the child. Parents get in a trap of being a principal figure to a child that when they say something, it is expected of the child to quickly understand them but in many cases children end up just doing what they think the parent meant even though it is not.

A parent who communicates with love and affection to a child is most likely to achieve the best results because the line is clear and open not hazy or engaged. It takes a lot of patience to have good communication skills.

To a certain extent a parent needs to be approachable for any kind of situation that a child faces. It is sad that because sometimes we treat parenthood as a criminal court, anytime the children try to say things, we don't listen carefully when they speak.

Communication is two way, not only the parent is supposed to be heard, the children need to be listened to as well. My mother once send me to buy bread but she did not specify how many loaves of bread I was supposed to buy. So I went to the shops and bought bread that was equivalent to the money she had given to me.When I went back home, she realised I had bought five loaves of bread and she was angry with me for spending all the money. She had assumed that I would buy two loaves as my elder siblings used to. From that day on, whenever she send me to buy anything at all, she would make sure I have understood what I was supposed to buy, she would even write it down.

Listening to Children with the Heart

Many young children are raped, bullied, abused in different ways under the parents' nose and mostly by someone close to the family, someone that the parents trust. but because the children are afraid to report because of fear of being judged and being told it's your fault, they keep quiete and live with it for the rest of their lives. One thing is, once children bottle things up, it won't vanish until even death, something that could have been dealt with by the parents.

Still on communication, listening is not only with the ear but with the heart too, the heart plays a big role in communication. If we don't communicate and listen with the heart, it's most likely that we might overlook and ignore the most important things. The look in your child's eyes can tell you how they are feeling and most parents don't look their children in the eye when communicating.

Sometimes you hear children say, I don't want to stay with uncle or aunt or they frown and become withdrawn. That is an indication of something not so good happening to them.

This account is a true story and it's not a unique account, I believe there are a millions of children going through the same situation out there.

These parents entrusted their two children with their uncle, the father's brother, uncle had just come to town to live with them from the village. They were both working and lived a harmonious family life, they thought uncle had come at a very convenient time which meant they no longer had to rush from work to pick the kids and drop them home from school and perhaps ask the neighbor to check on them till they finish work.

So the uncle resumed the duties, he would go, fetch the children and play with them till the parents return after work. The older was a 10 year old boy and the younger was a 7 year old little girl. This went on perfectly for a while until evil thoughts began to surface in the uncle's mind. So every time he brought the children home, he would give some coins to the young boy to go to the shops and buy sweets and crisps with his friends.

This enabled him to stay with the young girl alone in the house, he repeatedly raped the little girl and would threaten that her parents would beat her up instead, so she kept it to herself. Day after day she tried to tell mum that she wanted her or dad to take her from school instead of uncle and she wanted to go and play at her friend's after school, but the parents assured her that uncle was only helping her and she had to appreciate that.

She said it again and again and again but the parents would not ask why nor would they bulge in. Poor little girl had to live with this nightmare for over a year and parents didn't notice at all.

One day she went to her friend's house during the weekend, the friend's mother noticed that she was not her usual self, because she was always bubbly and happy, this time she was withdrawn and she looked scared. The friend's mother took her aside and asked her what was the matter, she couldn't say for a long time and the friend's mother kept asking, she did not tire as her instincts were telling her something was not well.

After about three months of her friend's mother asking, she finally gathered the courage to tell her that she was being abused by the uncle for a long time but was afraid to tell the parents. The friend's mother embraced her, in tears and assured her that she was going to be alright. The matter was later investigated and not only did the uncle stole the little girl's pride, but he infected her with HIV. To the parents' shock.

1. Do you think as a parent, your communication with your children is good enough?

Technology Discipline

Gone are the days when the families would gather around the table, sit, chat, laugh and bond together in one without divided attention. More and more, the technology is evolving to the advantage of many aspects and to the disadvantage of family quality time.

From the parents to the children everyone is skyping, tweeting, and facebooking and more, it has gone to the extent that children now prefer to play games on the internet than going out there and play in the park with friends. Parents also spend a vast amount of time checking their facebook homepage to see what is happening to their friends and updating events, feelings and disappointments e.t.c.

This bug has creeped in and is here to stay. The scenario in homes where mum and dad has headphones and on you tube, elder children in their rooms on the internet, the baby watching cartoons, no one is there to care for each other. It is quite disturbing to even learn that children end up getting hooked up with pedophiles and abusers through this.

Parents still need to make sure the bonding time with children is still established even though modern technology will continue evolving and making it even more easier and cheaper to be on social networking sites more than studying or bonding with family.

The first step is to accept the situation and try to put a defined time for cyber networking which is strict to every member of the family including mum and dad. The internet is so vast and you can access pretty much anything you want on it. There is also the need to put in place a monitoring tool of what children are watching on the net, it is possible to block access to certain material on the children's computers. You can contact the nearest IT specialists to make control features on websites to be navigated by children, blocking sites with pornographic material and online dating sites. It is also possible to do that on their phones, this will also reduce your children meeting with strangers online and getting lured into other malice.

Bonding Time with Children—The Importance

Bonding with children is as important as drinking water, we drink water because we feel that the body needs and depend on it, and it irrigates our body for the body to function well. Equally to the children, they need parents' undivided attention to feel adequate and for their happiness. It is of vital importance for their overall health—physical, emotional and psychological. It is loving unconditionally, when you bond with your children, you have to develop a mutual emotional connection. The way you treat and behave with children gives them comfort and it helps establish closeness.

Understanding the importance of bonding and methods as a parent helps you and your children to forge a great relationship ahead. Not only is bonding important to children, it also enables the parent to know their children better. We can bond with our children in different ways. This is one aspect without a price tag on it. The children need to feel the sense of belonging, they need to feel the love and affection from their parents, it gives them good confidence as individuals.

SOME WAYS TO BOND WITH CHILDREN

- Playing games
- Talking softly
- Kind and love gestures to each other i.e. a kiss on the cheek
- Watching fun programmes on TV
- Going for walks
- Just talking
- Laughing together
- Singing
- Doing house chores together
- Going to outdoor programmes

INSTILLING GOOD VALUES IN CHILDREN

Values once again are an investment that parents give to their children. These values are permanent; the children stay with them wherever they are till they die. When I was young, I had a brother who had a very comfortable life and every time he came home he would bring us some new clothes and other goodies for the family. The first thing we were concerned about as children whenever he came home was, 'what did he bring for me'. It went on and on and on for a long time and in our minds when we saw him, we no longer cared much about him but about what he brought us.

As we understand that in life everybody has their good harvest time and their bad harvest time. For whatever reason at some point, my brother's material life changed drastically, apparently he had lost his job and the luxuries he had were now things of the past.

When he came home in that cloudy situation, he could only manage to bring a cabbage, one cabbage which I think costed the equivalent of 20p.He got home, he did not have a car anymore, so that meant no running to the boot. As children we were sad and wondered why brother had not brought the usual goodies, we obviously did not understand.

When he was about to leave, going back to town, it was a family tradition at my home that when everyone was leaving or travelling from home the whole family would gather, sing and pray for God to be guide. Before we sang and prayed, my father said to my brother,'Son,we are really grateful that you came to see us, we know things might not be going well but we do not bother whether you bring us anything or not, the most important thing for us is to see you'.

This touched me a lot and it was a lesson to me up to now I personally have learnt not to just value material possessions but to value a person, another human being as they are whether they are poor or rich. It is a value that was instilled in me through a different situation.

It doesn't only take the parents to verbally address the values to children, but also the action, the little gestures, love, harmony, good approach to things and situations, being proud of who you are, what have you. Come to think of it, if we spend most of our time talking, gossiping about how the lady next door doesn't know how to mix and match clothes and shoes, we express our hate to others, we insult and use bad language, even if we go to church, after church we comment negatively about others. Children are like CCTV cameras, they record everything and later in life these values you gave to your children will surface to the whole world, they seize to shine as they should.

We communicate values to our children through words and action. How we solve issues and how we address others, if we are positive then our positivity will shine through our children.

ENVIRONMENTAL INFLUENCE

Children are exposed to a variety of environmental variables that can place them at risk of anti-social behaviour. The environment has a large bearing on the mentality and conduct of children, children are exposed to different environments, if you take children from the rural areas and children from the urban areas, suburbs, streets, high streets, and you will find that their tone and conduct is different. The way they perceive life in general is different.

Every environment has its advantages and disadvantages but even though children are influenced largely by the environment that doesn't mean we can stereotype environment because we come back to individuality, personal conduct which is quite influenced by parents, siblings, school, or church etc.

If children live in a neighbourhood or home where most children or parents are in the streets drinking alcohol, smoking, gossiping and doing prostitution, they can get lured into that and think that is the way of life. The frequency and intensity of certain malice behaviour within the children's environment can cause a lot of damage. There are very few fortunate cases where children actually shun doing malice in such environments and do better in life.

The school environment can mould children in a way but this is where children are also exposed to friends who either have good conduct or bad conduct. Generally the teenagers are most affected by the school environment because of peer pressure.

The trend of competitiveness plays a bigger influence at this stage, the dressing, boyfriends, girlfriends, sex. I have heard quite a lot of young girls and boys who bully others because they are still virgins; they have not yet experienced sexual relations with someone. It troubles many children and many a times because they want to feel that they belong they end up indulging.

If a parent sensitizes children of the advantages and disadvantages of practicing and not practicing such things as pre-marital sex, drinking, smoking e.t.c this may help the children to make informed decisions. Which is why it is important to help children feel confident with who they are rather than following what the next person is doing.

There are many children who find themselves becoming gangsters not because they want but to satisfy their peers and to look cool.

Maltreatment is a generic term; it maybe used to describe physical abuse, verbal abuse, emotional abuse, sexual abuse and psychological abuse. Maltreatment is an example of a dysfunctional interaction between parents and children. An environment where maltreatment is high can lead to promiscuity, becoming suicidal and turn children into unconfident and withdrawn individuals.

In a nutshell, no matter where you come from, it is not far from doing good because doing good is right in front of you.

Social interaction

Interaction in children plays a very big role in their growth, children need to have people they associate, interact and play with. They need to have people outside family circles whom they socialize with in different settings, at school, at home, kindergarten and any other place. For young babies it helps develop their motor skills and when older it contributes to the development of self confidence, sense of love, sharing and fellowship.

However as much as social interaction is so important, it also comes with its own challenges. It depends on who the children choose to interact and socialize with, which makes it worthwhile or not so worthwhile. The parent's role in this aspect is trying to encourage the children to choose good friends, friends with good behavior and conduct, friends who don't hang around bullies, thieves, promiscuous people and all other negative characters that only bring trouble. Although your child has a cell phone and email, you may find it difficult to track who he/she is friends with.

With social media and "friends" online, chat rooms, instant and text messaging and internet enabled cell phones; it is hard to know to whom your child is talking to. Building a strong relationship with your child is important to improve communication between you both. You will be more aware of things that may be bothering them such as cyber bullying, stress in the family and other things that they should not deal with on their own.

It is important for parents to know the people that the children choose to socialize with. Invite your children's friends to your home and talk to them, try to understand their family background, lifestyle, their beliefs and aspirations. This enable better understanding and an opportunity to learn whether they are good friends or not.

Sometimes our children hang out with people who abuse drugs or of a violent nature and our children might actually be lured into it and may want to experiment. It is in the experimenting that the children might get hooked and addicted to certain vices not so beneficial to their lives. It is therefore important that as much as children need friends, we have to make sure that they find friends who build them not destroy them.

Sleepovers

1. Is it a good idea that our children go for sleepovers?
2. What are the most important factors to consider when sending children for sleepovers?

Factors To Consider When sending Children For Sleepovers

- Have adequate knowledge of the children's friends, their behavior and values, how they comport.
- Make sure you have met the family before, that includes everyone who lives at your child's friend's house, and are satisfied with their lifestyle and conduct.
- Verify with the friend's family if they know of the sleepover arrangement.
- Drop the child at the house if possible and pick them at combined time.
- Give some advice on how to behave at the friend's house before they leave.

SEX TALK

Talking about sex to our children is obviously not a walk in the park, it is not easy. It's not comfortable for anyone involved—parents are afraid of it, children are mortified by it—which is probably why the talk so often comes after the consequences. In the latest study on parent-child talks about sex and sexuality, researchers found that more than 40% of adolescents had had intercourse before talking to their parents about safe sex, abstinence till marriage, sexually transmitted diseases.

Technically talking to children about sex is raising awareness of the reality that is in humans and in the world and trying to address the most important aspects to look out for. There are a few things to consider when talking about sex to children, the approach, convenient place and being well informed of what to talk about.

As much as it is difficult for a parent to approach children on this aspect, this is so because whether we believe it or not, children are exposed to a diversity of information on this regard, friends, peers, classmates, magazines, television and any other form of media that communicates sex material and info-internet. Our children are not immune to this and it is much better that they receive this education at home to guide them through external pressures.

Most children are starting to be sexually active at as young as 9, 10 and mostly they get trapped in the emotions and feeling and sometimes just to look cool to their friends. They don't understand what goes on and the after effects per se and that's when we see unwanted pregnancies surfacing, STDs that can end up killing them.

Talking about sex to children in some cultures and traditions is regarded as a taboo, most parents and the community might think it actually drives children into indulgence. This on the other hand can result in many young children being impregnated, getting Sexually Transmitted Infections, fail to finish studies and other consequences that comes with it. A lot can happen to children if they are not informed on this subject.

It is very important to know what exactly a parent should discuss when it comes to the talking about sex.

1. **When**: The appropriate time and age is important, this is dependent on generation I guess but the best time to talk to children about sex is from 9 years. At 9 years most children already understand a bit or a lot about sex.

2. **How**: As mentioned before, the how part is most challenging. The way a parent approaches a child and the topic is very important in making them understand and believe in you. Talking to children in a more private place and trying to start by asking if they know or understand anything about sex. A parent must always show confidence in what they are saying so that the child may trust and believe you more that his/her peers.

3. **What**: What exactly do we want to communicate to the children about sex? When we commence the talk, it is pertinent that we understand the most important points which are, understanding their sexuality, understanding the opposite sex, what sex is and the best stage that one is expected of indulging in sex, the consequences of pre-marital sex, protection. With teenagers it is pertinent to highlight the issue of unwanted pregnancies and sexually transmitted

Infections. This is broad and each parent can choose to talk more relating to their religious, cultural and family beliefs.

4. **Why**: Do I really need to do this? It is a question that parents might ask themselves. Yes it is your responsibility parent. It is better for a child to later say but my mum, my dad told me about this than to be faced with questions like, would it have made a difference when the water is already under the bridge. It is better for children to learn from you than external peers and media.

Handling finances
with children

Everybody in the world is worried and toiling to earn some money in order to put food on the table, sending children to school, buying clothes, sustaining other needs in the home. Whilst money brings stability and happiness to any family, money also brings a lot of grief, hate, confusion, instability, and unhappiness to families too.

One man in a remote area in Africa was the main bread winner in the family and for all the needs of the house, the mother or the children had to tell him that Pa, we need this, Pa, we need that, and he would take it from his pocket and give it to them. This became routine in the family that one day one of his children was playing in the river and was attacked by a crocodile, and he needed urgent attention, as usual the family waited for the father to come back home so that they would ask for money to rush the child to the hospital.

On this particular day, there was a hold up in traffic because of another accident as he worked in town. The family waited and waited for quite a long time, all this time, the child was bleeding, they tried to tie cloths around the affected areas, tried to seek help from neighbours but no one could offer financial help, the hospital was more that 10miles from that remote area. Way back then, not many people had mobile phones or cars.

After a long exhausting wait the father got home, and he saw the sad look on everyone's face and realized one of his sons was lying down almost unconscious, he was alarmed and his wife told him about the ordeal, they then rushed to carry him in a wheelbarrow to the bus station. When they finally got to the hospital, they received bad news that the child had suffered heavy loss of blood and as a result he lost his life.

Many a times it so happens that a parent might want to be in control of the finances by keeping everything to themselves to the extent that even when there are emergencies in their absence, the other members don't know what to do.

When finances are not handled transparently in the family, it brings confusion and assumption that maybe dad or mum always has money, the demands also grow every time because the children think there is more in that pocket or in that handbag.

Therefore it is quite pertinent that a parent involves children in their financial budgeting, this gives them a sense of financial responsibility and they also learn to prioritize. You will realize that if you do your family budget together, there are no unforeseen demands throughout the month.

It is also very important that the children understand the importance of working hard, even if one is a millionaire or billionaire; the children still need to work hard in their lives because money comes and money goes. You might be rich today and poor tomorrow.

So, if you teach your children to work for their money then they will not feel the gap if things change. They will learn to work hard for their money.

Take a good example Mitchell Obama; I was touched to learn that she gives only 1 dollar for pocket money to her children. Not only was I touched by that, but it clearly shows that being financially stable does not mean spoil children, the children still need to understand that you earn money not just spend it. This shows how important the way we handle finance issues in our homes is.

Tips to Handling Finances with Children

- Do the monthly budgeting together with children
- Teach children to identify the priorities first rather than wants
- Analyse your spending periodically as a family and see whether you have savings.
- Teach children to save even using tins to put coins
- Teach children to live within your means

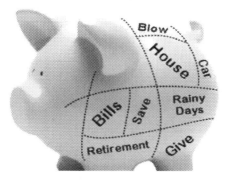

MISTAKES DON'T DEFINE YOU AS A PARENT

Everybody makes mistakes and from them we should grow to be even better people, our past mistakes don't mean anything, it is how you choose to handle them that matters. Many parents sit in a boat and say, who am I to discipline my children, I did worse in the past. Sometimes we live in a society and community where people know what we did wrong in the past and we end up having fear to even tell our children right from wrong.

It reminds me of one of Joel Osteen's books, where he highlighted that many banks nowadays operate a two door system which when you open the first one,you will need to close it completely for the access door to open.So,parents need to close the doors of their past mistakes inorder for the new and better horizons to open.

A parent was entrusted to take care of children and try as much as possible to bring the best out of these children. The confusion, hurt, grief and more that the parents face in this journey is only normal and it should never take the best from us, rather we have to rise above all challenges and applaud ourselves for the job well-done.